He Cheated
Get The Hell Up!

A Quick Get Your Ass Up And Go Guide
After Being Cheated On

Samantha Peavy

He Cheated Get The Hell Up!: A Quick Get Your Ass Up And Go Guide After Being Cheated On
Samantha Peavy
Print ISBN: 979-8-9892562-3-5
Copyright 2024 by PIAOTT Publishing & Graphic Design LLC.

PI\OTT

PIAOTT Publishing & Graphic Design LLC.
Chicago, IL
www.piaottpublishing.com

This is dedicated to every woman or man that has been cheated on; rather you decided to stay or Get The Hell Up, this quick guide is for you.

To every broken, bitter, angry, pissed-off woman that just found out your man, husband, fiancée and the like cheated on you, may this layer of my lasagna lens bring healing and wholeness to the new you.

When Life Throws You Lemons, Make Lasagna

~Sam The Lasagna Lady

move forward

growing.

progressing.

accelerating.

advancing.

continuing.

Focused movement; the resilience in your life's Lasagna.

~Sam The Lasagna Lady

Table of Contents

"The church is a hiding place
for men to wear sheeps clothing."

Olive Barnabus,
A Seasoned Woman of God

A Note from Sam

Girl, whether you are in the five-fold ministry/dimension or a woman who loves being at home taking care of your family, you've been cheated on. You may have just found out that you married a cheater, serial cheater, and/or narcissist. Nonetheless, you can make it! Riding the waves is an interesting thing. Sufferers know what to do depending on the condition of the water at the beach where they're waiting for that wave.

Let's think about lasagna. The noodles, to be exact. Some lasagna pasta noodles have ridges that look like waves on each side of the noodle where the middle of it is smooth. Funny how waves on a noodle can be a guide to thrust you forward. On Christmas Day 2022, I found out I was married to a serial cheating mf'er. I expressed my disappointment, forgave him right away, and moved on.

The waves you're about to ride are intentionally purposed to guide you to your new you. Be open, ladies, to loving again. Ride the wave that has been strategically put together for you. Just like that suffer, you'll know when to catch the wave and ride. Examine every detail of the wave; the wind, breeze, the mist from the water brushing against your face, the smoothness of the ride, the clarity of the water, and the scent of the ocean. Observe your attitude and how this wave made you feel. So, ride the wave.

Lasagna has an interesting way of showing us what life is about. First, the water is cold in the pot, then boiled, and the noodles get the shock to soften so that they can be stretched and layered in the entrées pan. In life, we get pulled, stretched, bent out of shape (emotional eating), overly stretched/stressed, etc. Lasagna noodles have the same elasticity as we do. Only it's applied to one of this world's favorite entrées, Lasagna. If you overcook the noodles, you have a starchy mess and overly stretched noodles; if it is slightly boiled more than Al dente, it's stretched but is still usable in the dish. However, if you boil your lasagna noodles perfectly, they have an ideal consistency and are ready to be layered and further baked with other ingredients. The ingredients compliment one another. Now, that is a perfect bite, even after being baked in the oven.

As you discover the powerful new you embrace happiness like the cheese in the lasagna that sticks closely to and brings all the ingredients together. These ingredients in this powerful new you include wisdom, bravery, strength, love, and kindness. It is the cheese that holds all of it together. Be free to add as much as you want to your layered lasagna or, better yet, the new you. Have the courage to walk away from dead relationships that have dragged your ass with people that really don't like you, including your cheater. If he liked you, he would not have cheated (cheating is intentional, not an accident).

As you journey your badass in the adventure of the powerful new you, thank God for His many blessings, for leading you and enlarging your capacity. Include Him, and He will direct your paths. Below is a scripture from the book of wisdom, Proverbs.

Thank God every day, every moment.
He has an amazing journey for you.

~Sam The Lasagna Lady

1-2 My child, if you truly want a long and satisfying life,

never forget the things that I've taught you.

Follow closely every truth that I've given you.

Then you will have a full, rewarding life.

3 Hold on to loyal love and don't let go,

and be faithful to all that you've been taught.

Let your life be shaped by integrity,

with truth written upon your heart.

4 That's how you will find favor and understanding

with both God and men—

you will gain the reputation of living life well.

Wisdom's Guidance

5 Trust in the Lord completely,

and do not rely on your own opinions.

With all your heart rely on him to guide you,

and he will lead you in every decision you make.

6 Become intimate with him in whatever you do,

and he will lead you wherever you go.

7 Don't think for a moment that you know it all,

for wisdom comes when you adore him with undivided

devotion and avoid everything that's wrong.

8 Then you will find the healing refreshment

your body and spirit long for.

The Meaning of Courage

Courage (Greek meaning added: Biblehub.com)

To radiate warm confidence (because warm-hearted)

Refers to God bolstering the believer, empowering them with a bold inner-attitude (to be "of good courage")

For the believer, *2293/tharséō* ("showing boldness") is the result of the Lord infusing His strength by His inworking of faith.

Showing this unflinching, bold courage means living out the inner confidence (inner bolstering) that is Spirit-produced.

means 'have confidence, courage, be unafraid,' with the nuance determined by the context.

To be bold

The ability to do something that frightens you.

Mental or moral strength to venture, persevere, and withstand danger, fear, or difficulty.

The ability of facing and dealing with anything recognized as dangerous, difficult, or painful, instead of withdrawing from it, quality of being fearless or brave, valor.

Basically, courage is the quality of a confident character not to be afraid or intimidated easily, but without being incautious or inconsiderate.

Chapter One

Bound Or Free

"I pray that your heart
be enlightened
to escape the enemy's
hidden secret traps
of darkness."

S o, you just found out what your gut has been saying to you all along; that your spouse, fiancée, man, or whatever the relationship dynamic; is a cheating mf'er.

Now what? You have so many emotions running through your mind, heart, and head. You want to do damage to his car, hurt him physically, and the like. PAUSE for a moment and examine why God allowed you to find out.

It's certainly not because of the cheater. This is for you to escape bondage by allowing God to show you how to leave being wise as a serpent and harmless as a Dove. Vengeance belongs to God, not you.

Your thoughts should not be consumed with the detail of this mf'er, "Fuck him!" As a relative of mine expressed to me in a quick chat. "Thanks, Gayle, for that and for me sharing that small part of our conversation."

God does not want you isolated to the agenda of a man who does not know how to treat you. So, girl, don't you feel sorry for him. He is going to go through the physical emotion of recycling remorse, which I talk about in chapter four. There will be gifts, flowers, candy, and blissful words you have longed to hear. Bottom line – Move Forward!!! Allow the voice of bravery to speak to you. The big girl bitch power you got inside you that's been screaming for you to gain courage and Get The Hell Up out of this hidden bondage.

Cheaters have one agenda, to keep you bound. This should frustrate and even anger you more. Yes, you've been in bondage, no matter the faith dynamic you're in with a relationship with God or not. You've been shouting and dancing depending on the type of church house you're connected with; BOUND.

BOUND DEFINED

The word bound has many definitions, which I'll share below. If you're crying right now because you just found out your spouse has been cheating with one or several women or even men, you have 10 minutes to do so.

When I left my cheating ass spouse, I stayed at a hotel for 33 days, and a woman, we'll call her Roxy, shared the 10-minute cry with me. She said she would tell her children who were upset or hurt in relationships that they had 10 minutes to cry about it and then move forward. Then Roxy stated, "Sam, you got 10 minutes to cry about this." Ladies, your 10-minute cry is going to be monumental in moving forward. This is a crucial cry so you don't waste unnecessary molecules of your brain on the cheater. This propels you to your purpose, opening your ear to hear the Lord God speak to you.

The word bound is commonly used as an adjective but can also function as a verb, a noun, or a suffix. Let's explore in detail how being bound has affected your mental and spiritual health.

BOUND implies being bound or determined. Your cheater had you bound, and he was determined to continue cheating until you found out.

- **To be seriously intending to do something.**
  Your cheater intentionally intended to keep your neck under his feet. Other people gleaning at your relationship may have known you were bound to leave the cheating mf'er one day. Don't get me wrong; forgive him and move

on. Just because you've forgiven does not mean you need or have to remain in a toxic relationship.

- **Tied with cord, rope, or string.**

Although you may not have been physically tied up, your destiny was strung and tied up. You can't see this because it is or was a form of bondage your cheater has or had you under. However, God had preserved you in a holding pattern until you activate forward movement.

Forms of bondage can be his control over the finances, control over everything, devaluing your worth as a woman, pulling you like a puppet string to cover his marital affairs with other women or men. This type of bondage is designed to destroy your mental state. Girl, Get The Hell Up and reclaim your own thinking. Cheaters want you to second guess yourself, keeping your thinking distorted by constant turmoil that distributes thoughts to your heart, soul, and spirit. No wonder you've been unable to think because your cheater(s) grip consumed your thought patterns.

- **To move quickly with large jumping movement**

This definition of bound can go in two different wavelengths.

1. You are now moving forward quickly with big girl; bad-ass lady moves to get away from the cheating mf'er.
2. The cheater moved so quick that it was hard for you to keep up with his moves as a pretend pimp. His moves capture weak women who are impressed and subdued by him, but you are the one who suffered the blow of his infidelity.
3. The women and/or men he cheated with are not

important. Do not waste your time on the details of this mf'er and all the people he's cheated with. Instead, focus your attention and attitude on being free and your purpose. Keep yourself up. Pamper yourself, take a nice long bath or shower, ignore phone calls, emails, and social media platforms.

4. Be kind to yourself and, more importantly, patient.

5. Look for a handpicked attorney led by God, set up a free consultation, and follow through when you decide what to do.

6. Obtain funds from the bank after you leave, then remove yourself from all joint accounts.

7. Let the cheater know that it is the least he could do to provide you with money for living. He's already doing sumthin' strange to give change to his Ho, Ho, Ho's, along with his affection.

8. Embrace being free and able to think clearly. That's the first part. With this new bravery, your mind needs nurturing from the curse you've been under.

9. Decide what friendships are necessary in your new big move. Only share your moves with people you trust.

10. Not everyone is for you since you left the cheating mf'er. That's real!

11. If y'all have kids together, he will use them as a manipulating tool. Please don't allow him to control you any longer. Find out your state's laws concerning this matter.

12. Talk to your attorney about your do's and don'ts, but if you and your children are being punched around,

take the necessary steps for protection according to your state.

13. Stay free, don't go back. You don't need him, you need GOD!

14. Consider your health. The longer you stay in a toxic relationship, the more you open yourself to sicknesses or diseases, depending on the length of your bondage in the relationship.

   Your health is important. Jeremiah 33:6 Nevertheless, I will bring health and healing to it; I will heal my people and will let them enjoy abundant peace and security.

God has plans for you beyond this toxic relationship.

"For I know the plans I have for you, 'declares the LORD,' plans to give you hope and a future. Then you will call on me and come and pray to me, and I will listen to you."
Jeremiah 29:11-12 (NIV) biblehub.com

• **To forbid, prohibit, to bind, fasten with chains.**
(Biblical meaning from King James Bible dictionary)

It's hard to believe that someone you loved and thought loved you carefully with intention wants/wanted to prevent you from being happy, loved, and successful and did not want you to be free in the relationship.

On Christmas day, 2022, I found out that the man I married and thought to be the one was mf'ing cheater with several women at the same time. Immediately, a scripture appeared to me. **"The wise woman builds her house, but with her own hands the foolish one tears hers down."** Proverbs 14:1 (NIV) So, I chose to forgive him right away. He didn't know I knew yet since he had fallen asleep. Late Christmas Eve, while on the computer, I made a horrible discovery. I came across and obtained all these emails, pictures, and text messages between him and strange women. The Bible says in Proverbs 6:32, **"But the man who commits adultery is an utter fool, for he destroys himself."** I could not believe that he'd decided to betray our marital relationship.

Later, on Christmas day, he became angry because I found out. Before heading out, I told him I forgave him and shared my disappointment. He didn't want to accept my forgiveness but rather chose to assault me when we were on our way out the door. To my disbelief, I defended myself by pushing him in the face to get away from him. I filed the necessary report as neither of the stories matched. Nonetheless, I moved out.

Upon arriving at the place I had fled to, two pictures were hanging on the walls. One was of a man bound with chains, and the other, on an adjacent wall, was of the same man free from those chains. I didn't like that and expressed it to the person I was living with. Although I was grateful to God for blessing me with a place to stay, I didn't like the wall art in my new bedroom. Even after weeks of living there, I could not look at the free man. Instead, I identified myself with the wall of him being bound.

I cried for nearly a month at this art, reminding me that I was under a curse in that relationship, bound with chains of his affairs, infidelities, emotional cheating, the soul ties he allowed in our marriage, and his constant narcissistic control. I sobbed so much I never paid attention to the other picture, but one day, early in the morning, God allowed me to look at the other picture on the wall. See, I was moving forward with big leaps but still reminiscing about my constant bondage. This is the morning he broke free from the chains of his bondage. I embraced the other picture and began to look through the lens I call "The Lasagna Lens."

Well, that didn't last very long because I decided after several months to go back and try to work things out according to the verbal agreement he and I had. Of course, I learned later that it was all talk to get me back. However, my mind was free from his bullcrap this time.

After a while, the Holy Spirit began ministering to me to move forward. I prayed and prayed and always got the same answer, "Move forward." "Keep moving forward."

God is so good that He even sent people (some I didn't know) my way with the same message. Thank You, Jesus! So, I did just that. God knows what and who He wants in our lives and when. I ran slowly but by faith in a hurry I moved forward. That is when I became homeless. This was a great thing! I trusted the Lord and moved forward in the direction guided by Him, God the Father, God the Son, and God the Holy Spirit.

This guide won't be popular with people around you who are bound by religious mindsets. I've met women and men who were told to stay by those bound with this type of mindset. The ones I met decided to leave and escape being cheated on while being beaten physically, emotionally, and spiritually. If you are reading this book and bound by a religious mindset, get delivered. God does not want you stuck in religion. He's waiting for a relationship with you, not religion with you.

The day I finally moved out was long but liberating. I moved into a hotel. Ladies, all the weight of bondage in this toxic relationship was broken. God removed those weights, like the picture on the wall. He allowed me to see that I would not be bound to a toxic relationship. I listened and hearkened to the voice of the Lord. I moved forward!

THOUGHTS TO PONDER

If you are in danger, please get the proper protection according to your state. Moving forward might be challenging. If you decide to leave, consider the following:

• Secure an Online USPS account. You'll be able to see your incoming mail. If the cheater decides to withhold it from you, the necessary proof is in your USPS emails.

• Change every password that you're using together.

• If you have honors discounts for hotels or airline rewards programs, change the passwords and telephone numbers connected to those accounts.

"Now, the Lord is the Spirit, and where the Spirit of the Lord is, there is liberty." 2 Corinthians 3:17

Life Through The Lasagna Perspective Lens:

There's nothing like piecing lasagna together. Enjoy the harvest of great conversation and friends as you partake in the entrée. Pieces of you have been fragmented and broken under this relationship. Take those pieces back and balance them with a new you.

Note that in your layers of lasagna perspective, your skin will look new, your conversations will shift, and your circle will become smaller. More lasagna for yawl to share together. LOL! A Lasagna Perspective lens to life sets you free to taste something different, opening new frames and structures to build upon and explore who you are. Enjoy building your new lasagna in these layers, your powerful new you!

You Can Breathe Again!
~Sam The Lasagna Lady™

Chapter Two

Submission To Silence

"I pray your words activate faith moves that align with God's purpose for you, and that your thinking be sound."

God has a plan, and being still and knowing that God is fighting for you is all the fight you need.

I recall the first time he told me to "Get the fuck out of his car." It was frightening because I didn't know where this was coming from. He also said other things, but I give no glory or energy to that. I quickly realized that I must *Submit To Silence*.

Over time, I noticed that my words were devalued even in the face of masked pretense. I accepted this silence and used it to my advantage. I'd sing songs to avoid the lack of intimacy, meaning candid conversation. All the years of being married, I had to beg for a hug or kiss. I'd cry myself to sleep and in silence when we visited people together. He'd give me hug and a kiss or two, in front of others. Although it was phony, I accepted what I could get because when we returned to our place, things reverted back to silence and controlled affection.

Being silent opens your ears to hear, your eyes to see, and all your senses to intertwine. Your ears begin to see, your eyes begin to hear, and so on. Quietness increases your level of sensitivity. Submitting to silence or being silenced by the man I married had its benefits and not-so-good moments.

One day, I purchased a box of 3x5 cards that read "Stop talking". I placed some of the cards in my kitchen as a reminder to stop talking. It saved me because anything I said in a conversation was unimportant, and I would be devalued if I could not remember everything he said. Oh, by the way, I have a Traumatic Brain Injury

(TBI). So, my memory was very challenged. I couldn't remember something as simple as taking my vitamins seconds after taking them. So, to remember the details of all our chats was impossible.

I soon learned to put up a united front around others. I'm sure people assumed we were this wonderful couple. If they only knew, they were way off. I spent many times quietly in my washroom, sometimes eating dinner. I'd been belittled enough for the day; the washroom was a treat. I'd pray for the happiness of someone, even though I was not happy. He would often tell me, "If you're not happy, leave." **WOW!**

In many instances, his frustration would rise at me for being quiet. I did not know what to say, so I'd just be silent, thinking, doesn't he know he is the reason I rarely talk?

If you're in that place of silence, it's not a bad thing. Your reasons for getting there may be different, but your discernment will increase. God will reveal more to you because you're quiet or still now. He's got your attention to provide direction to minister to the hurt you feel. Being in that place allows you to hear your voice audibly.

The disadvantages of submitting to silence do not outweigh the benefits. Strategy happens when you're silent. A strategist is successful at being strategic in the fields of their study. Intercessors can intercede effectively with a strategy in place. It often takes being silent. Here are a few things to think about in your "being quiet" time.

- Think about your happiness and what that looks like for you and your children.
- Think about new levels of intimacy with God. One benefit of submitting to silence is that it can be felt with your heart. It's a special bond shared with God because it's altogether personal in your relationship with Him. You'll get to know and always be able to hear Him. **"Man shall not live on bread alone but on every word that**

proceeds out of the mouth of God." Matthew 4:4

- You will display strength and take action, even in being silent. **"By smooth words he will turn to godlessness that who act wickedly toward the covenant, but the people who know the God will display strength and take action."** Daniel 11:32

- So much movement is happening on your behalf, even though not visible to the eye.

- Your silence is strengthening your growth in listening to Father God, as Jesus did. All day, even in your sleep, your listening fortitude is being strengthened. **"Then the Lord came and stood and called as other times, 'Samuel! Samuel!' and Samuel said, 'Speak for Your servant is listening.'"** I Samuel 3:10

THINGS TO PONDER

To continue in the intimate walk with the Lord God, consider these actions:

- Embrace the intimate relationship with God as personal.

- Talk with Him. Tell Him about your day. Cry with Him and laugh with Him.

- Be patient and kind again to yourself.

- Do not allow the spirit of idolatry to block your intimacy with God. This is a critical part of your moving forward.

- Listen well.

- Pray and read the Bible.

- Be open to being vulnerable with Him. God knows you; get to know Him.

- **"Never doubt God's mighty power to work in you and**

accomplish all this. He will achieve infinitely more than your greatest request, your most unbelievable dream, and exceed your wildest imagination! He will outdo them all, for his miraculous power constantly energizes you." Ephesians 3:20 (The Passion Translation)

Life Through The Lasagna Perspective Lens:

When lasagna is baking in the oven, you may not hear every sizzle and sound of the ingredients. However, just because you don't hear it does not mean there is no movement.

Your intimacy with the Lord can be as hot as an oven, causing movement in your heart for the purpose He has for you. Similarly, like a pan of Lasagna, the cheese connects the pasta noodles to the sauce and other ingredients heated in the oven, igniting movement and creating new levels of freedom in the entrée.

God the Father, Son, and Holy Spirit enjoy and are delighted at your intimacy with Him.

Chapter Three

Embrace Your New Beginning

"Gratitude
The quality of being thankful.
A readiness to show appreciation
for and to return kindness
Giving of thanks, gratefully,
gratitude, thankfulness,
thanks, thanksgiving,
The giving of thanks
for God's grace."

Weights are interesting. They help build muscle for strength and endurance and include dumbbells or barbells to help you train the muscles. Scientifically, a weight is the force acting on an object due to gravity. The weight of an object depends on the gravitational field at the point in space where the object is. Weight is a force, which means that it has direction as well as magnitude. The weight carried has direction. Ponder on that!

Weights are also heaviness, a load, pressure, a burden, or tonnage—weight in tons, especially for cargo or freight. One of the definitions in Greek meaning is that weight is equivalent to authority. To have authority and influence.

You're ready for your new beginning now that your muscles have been trained; they're conditioned to endure. You might have had the Band-Aid snatched off you to find out you're married or connected to deception, betrayal, or a cheating m'fer. The direction you face clearly outlines what you must do to reach a specific place and begin developing the new you. As we learned in the Greek definition, weight is equivalent to authority.

Your muscles are lean due to all the conditioning and training of the weights you carried from the cheater. How? You carried the weight of his deception, betrayal, his Ho Ho Ho's, and more while he blamed you for all of his hatred toward women and narcissistic behavior. Girl, you're tougher than you think! You've gained endurance and stamina at the stress of the weights you carried.

The magnitude of your direction propels you to advance in distance and quantity. He will not know what God is doing for, to, with, and in you. The size of your muscles has increased. Now, I don't mean just physically, but emotionally and mentally. The moment you decide to Get the Hell Up, things begin to move. Your faith in leaning into the Lord instead of your own emotions reveals forward movement. God is moved when we step out on faith and follow His direction.

A weight of heaviness is soul ties, and all the drama cheaters brought, including the witchcraft, voodoo, and all the spiritual wickedness in high places. Once you walk away, all the weight and heaviness you had to endure falls off you. I declare and decree it for you in the name of the Lord Jesus Christ and by the power of His blood.

Since your emotional, spiritual, and mental muscles have been trained to endure, they've been strengthened further to advance your quality of life and ability to do everyday activities. Your joints are protected from injuries the cheater caused and have become stronger.

Physically, we know what training does to the body and its muscles. However, I'm talking about how this particular training worked out for your good. Romans 8:28 says, **"And we know that in all things God works for the good of those who love him, who have been called according to his purpose."**

Remember, conditioning your muscles also deals with the extent to advance from the beginning. When you began your relationship, you were blind to any betrayal behind the scenes. You're open to being vulnerable in love, perhaps loving again if you've experienced heartbreak in prior relationships. You did not enter the relationship with caution. The lights were green, and you thought you were safe until you actually found out that he was not in the business of protecting you but rather protected the Ho Ho Ho's he cheated with. He did not have your back from day one.

It's helpful for you not to deceive yourself, thinking you can change him. Rather, change you and attract the man God has designed specifically for you. Don't carry the luggage of his turmoil into that new relationship when it comes.

In the meantime, know that you are leaner than you think and a more powerful you. Now you have lean muscles to enjoy your new beginning. You are no longer under a curse-led cheater. Congratulations on not going or looking back (more on this topic in Chapter 6).

Be aware that the cheating man that was once in your life is not going to want you to grow. After all, he never watered you with God's word, so why would he now?

"Husbands, love your wives, just as Christ loved the church and give himself up for her, to make her holy, cleansing her by the washing with water through the word, and to present her to himself as a radiant church, without strain or wrinkle or any other blemish, but holy and blameless."
Ephesians 5:25-27

When the weight of that toxic relationship falls off in the beginning, it's going to feel frightening. That's okay; embrace it and keep those muscles moving forward. Continue to condition them by being kind and patient with yourself. You've neglected yourself care for too long. Now it's time for you to heal, embrace your new beginning, and lean into God's love for you.

THINGS TO PONDER

- Develop a more intimate relationship with the Lord God.
- He wants you to get to know Him.
- STAY FREE; don't go back into bondage with the cheating m'fer.
- Think about what happiness means to you.

- Take a vacation or staycation; turn off your phone and DO YOU!
- Dance again. This relationship was designed to suck the life out of you, dance, girl, dance!
- Meet new people that God bless in your path.

"No weapon formed against you shall prosper, and every tongue which rises against you in judgment you shall condemn. This is the heritage of the servants of the LORD, and their righteousness is from Me," Says the LORD. Isaiah 54:17 NKJV

Life Through The Lasagna Perspective Lens

As you know, Lasagna is a layered dish that can be stacked with goodness as tall as you like. Even if there are only a few layers, the ingredients deepen the weight and depth of one of the world's favorite entrees.

There is nothing like the excitement of purchasing all the ingredients for your new lasagna dish: the pan, seasonings, pasta, and sauce (fresh, packaged, or jarred), cheese, and all the ingredients you desire.

Adventure, new intimacy, friends, and healthier relationships await you as you embrace your new beginning. So, enjoy the shopping list of adventure, love, and happiness in your life's Lasagna.

Be open to loving and falling in love again.
Don't allow the sting of a cheater to hinder the new man God will bring into your life, the one He has for you.

~Sam The Lasagna Lady™

Chapter Four

Remorseful Manipulation

"Once you've been
deflated enough
by your situation, perhaps
you'll have the courage
to Get the Hell Up
and leave!"

C heaters are experts in master manipulation. The mask to date, marry and cheat was a small fraction of his plan. I'll share the rest in Chapter 6 "Fleeing Chapters."

Once the infidelity/adultery has been revealed and your cheater is aware that you know, his manipulation clock is ticking. He's masterminding what he will tell others, something like, "she's just trippin' cause she found old emails to other women before we met." While your story is quite different. Don't waste your time on what he's deceived others to believe.

Remorseful defined:
- Filled with remorse; sorry; sad.
- Can be considered a part of emotional empathy.

Manipulation defined:
- The exercise of harmful influence over others

The sign of manipulation includes persistent excessive attention, love and flattery. Persistent despite boundaries, time pressure to get you to act. Does that sound familiar? Master manipulators know that they can go undetected by many people including you.

A few things to look out for, girl!

1. Avoid the voice of your emotions. Your emotion to a manipulator has a way of being subdued by the cheating mf'er.

2. Allow God to be your dependency. Lean into His love, mind and His strong arms. Stretch yourself further like a Lasagna

noodle and lean into His trust. **"Trust in the Lord with all your heart and lean not on your own understanding; in all your ways submit to him, and he will make your paths straight."** Proverbs 3:5-6

3. Cease from entertaining conversations with low self-esteem, the cheater and the people that try to keep you connected to the toxic relationship. If you have children together, understand they hurt too, but a part of them is happy you decided to Get the Hell Up. So, seek legal counsel. Cheater will use you children to further manipulate you, your new place and the powerful new you.

Manipulators and emotional manipulation are besties. Some of these manipulative behaviors include:

• Gaslighting: An example, a husband might manipulate his wife to declare her insane further in the relationship; pretending to care, he had the plan all along. However, he is the mastermind behind it so he can go onto the next woman or women for supply until he no longer needs her. If you are a cheater, you should think about avoiding marriage and continue to be with the low-level minded women that don't know how to think for themselves. They need you to puppet them, that's why they accept you being married while they cheat with you. Not because you are a hero to them, but because you have poisoned, their mind about your marital status, that, sadly, they actually believe you.

- Love Bombing: Girl RUN! This trait of narcissism or personality disorder in an unhealthy attachment to who you are. They enter the relationship and in one-day later they're in love and saying they love. RUN, RUN, RUN!!!

- Isolation: (1) A gossip betrays a confidence, but a trustworthy person keeps a secret. (2) For lack of guidance a nation falls, but victory is won through many advisers.

- Manipulators in their mastery, work to keep you from people and environments you feel safe in. Once he has manipulated you in great detail and from certain places of comfortability, the master manipulator can take control. This is unhealthy in a relationship.

THOUGHTS TO PONDER

People who manipulate others attack their mental and emotional sides to get what they want. The person doing the manipulating, called the manipulator, seek to create and imbalance of power and ultimate control.

The goal of the manipulation is to control the other person in order to get what the manipulator wants. It involves a wide scope of behaviors from being insidious to extremely subtle. **"The fear of man lays a snare, but whoever trusts in (God) the Lord is safe."** Proverbs 29:25

Life Through The Lasagna Perspective Lens:

- Never negotiate with a manipulator. It is a time waster. Often time recipes can be interconnected with other ingredients, but you'll never add a shoe as the base noodle in your Lasagna. It's as simple, the two do not go together in this dish. Let the Lasagna in your life, be a Lasagna.

- You are worthy of support. Your cheese people/real friend are always there to hold you up; in prayer, naturally, physically and supernaturally (Expounded in my book titled Life Through Lasagna Eyes: The Recipes for Life).

- Cheaters are good at what they do. They cheat in every relationship, even the ones they cheat with. Your brain does not need to entertain any molecules about the manipulative details of the women or men he's cheated with, girl, take the mindset of who cares and move forward. They'll never stop cheating and you definitely deserve someone extraordinarily better.

So let the Lasagna bake at the proper temperature of love, happiness and enjoy it not burnt, like the toxic relationship you walked away from.

Walk into the new boldness of you!

~Sam The Lasagna Lady

Chapter Five

Production of the New Chapters

"Don't let his opinion of you trump the journey of your new beginning."

Your faith causes things to move naturally and in the realm of the Spirit. If this is new to you and its your first time hearing this, it's okay.

"I planted the seed in your hearts, and Apollo's watered it, by it was God who made it grow Its not important who does planting, or who does the watering. What's important is that God makes the see grow. The one who plants and the one who water work together with the same purpose. And both will be rewarded for their own hard work." I Corinthians 3:6-8

New chapters! Yikes, what does that look like?

Your faith is a motivational force that propels you forward in the direction God desires. As your relationship grows with Him, you will understand His voice, how He speaks to you, and how the Holy Spirit guides you.

"Folly brings joy to one who has no sense, but whoever has understanding keeps a straight course. Plans fail for lack of counsel, but with many advisers, they succeed. A person finds joy in giving an apt reply—and how good is a timely word!" Proverbs 15:21-23

Seeds are programmed to grow. Have you ever planted a tomato in a garden, and it produced corn? No! The seed will produce its intended purpose. Production in your new chapters includes purposeful seeds and many seeds to grow.

You need to take action to ensure your growth. These include watering your seeds of purpose with prayer and connecting with the right people or organization to advance your new chapters. New chapters are not produced for those who settle for a cheating spouse or toxic relationships. Of course, settlers will have their own chapters because the cheater knows how to be clever and is doing just enough to get by. They've figured out how to finally manipulate the settler into staying while they continue to mastermind their cheating.

Again, we know God can turn things around. However, it's good to know that according to this family study in 2016, men are more likely than women to cheat: 20% of men and 13% of women reported that they've had sex with someone other than their spouse while married, according to data from the recent General Social Survey (GSS).

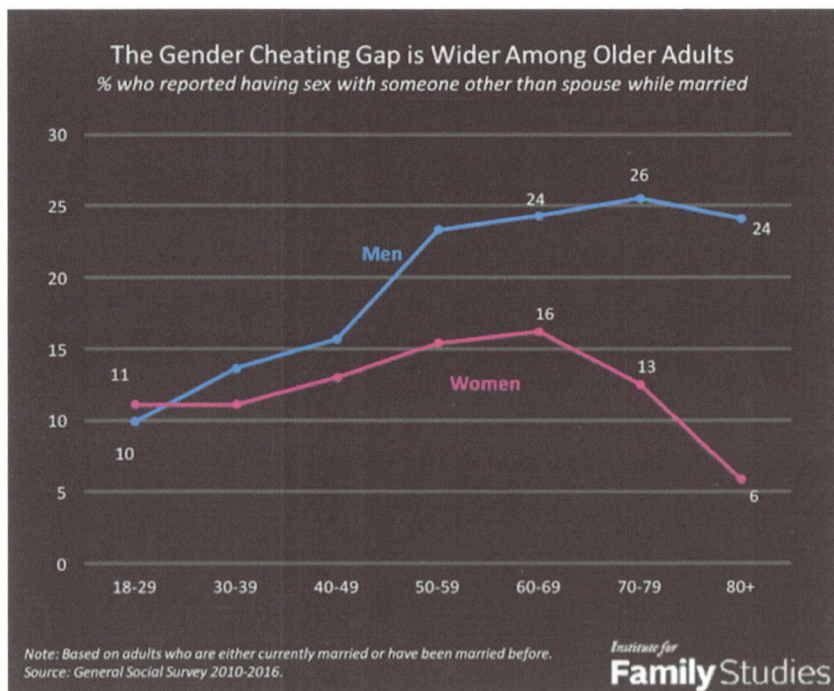

The Gender Cheating Gap is Wider Among Older Adults
% who reported having sex with someone other than spouse while married

Note: Based on adults who are either currently married or have been married before.
Source: General Social Survey 2010-2016.

Institute for **Family** Studies

Your new chapters bring stillness and quietness to help you navigate God's purpose and a new posture for you. New roots, production, and water - GIRL, you have spent too much time nurturing a dead relationship, dealing with a cheater, forgiving him over and over again. It's time you care for yourself, and if you have children, them too. This production ensures your posture is grounded in faith, courage, and a steady focus. Your posture is now framed with hope and belief in yourself. Remember, **"I can do all this through him who gives me strength."** Philippians 4:13

Treading on freshwater areas you were once afraid to walk is lighter. To walk in the deep of new water takes courage and faith. Your new chapters are filled with fresh perspectives, adventures, and so much more. You are conditioned with strong muscles and clothed with beauty and the aroma of your intimate relationship with the Lord. Your self-esteem has thickened with confidence.

THINGS TO PONDER

- Don't tell everyone your moves. Some things should remain with you. People love gossip and will pick sides; Even will side with the cheater. Be quiet when you need to be.
- Trust God's plan. He got you this far. Because you got this far, don't look back.

"Keep your lives free from the love of money and be content with what you have because God has said, "Never will I leave you, never will I forsake you." Hebrews 13:5

Life Through The Lasagna Perspective Lens:

As you continue in forward movement, bravery, and courage are the new sound in your layered Lasagna. The voice of poorly managed self-esteem has left the building. The low self-esteem that rehearses itself in your ear telling you to return to the cheater is a trick of the enemy. In this layer of Lasagna, creative thinking that comes from God Himself, layered with good medicine laughter and sandwiched with the joy of the Lord being your strength, makes for a fulfilling, purposeful journey of the production of your new chapters.

New Chapters are funny and sometimes quiet. A victory in quiet allows you to see beyond your circumstances.

~Sam The Lasagna Lady

Chapter Six

Fleeing Chapters

"Fleeing chapters means running away from the dangers of a toxic relationship."

Funny, new chapters ending often propel backward motion. Motivating someone to go back to a toxic relationship prolongs the new chapter.

The boat you once thought was safe has overturned with manipulation, misguided disguised hate, and secret sabotage, now ripens your awakening to move forward and swim safely to shore. Your journey to safety is not about the swim; it's about your trust in God for your happiness, freedom, and release from the damage of a toxic relationship or marriage. Ugh, here comes the mask to distort your thinking and hinder your dreams, with a hidden goal to discourage you and get you to quit what God called you to do.

"For we do not wrestle against flesh and blood, but against principalities, against powers, against the rulers of the darkness of this age, against spiritual hosts of wickedness in the heavenly places." Ephesians 6:12 NKJV

"The focus of my letter wasn't on punishing the offender but on getting you to take responsibility for the health of the church. So if you forgive him, I forgive him. Don't think I'm carrying around a list of personal grudges. The fact is that I'm joining in with your forgiveness, as Christ is with us, guiding us. After all, we don't want to unwittingly give Satan an opening for yet more mischief—we're not oblivious to his sly ways!" 2 Corinthians 2:11 Message Bible

Satan's device tactics are to put mis-guided suggestions and lies in our minds, that promote an unforgiving spirit among brethren. Toxic relationships don't begin that way for both involved but end with two people that needs to show forgiveness to themselves.

Unshifted waters in an ocean of love carries the boat of the two people in love. Their intimacy, laughter, and pure joy for each other; the songs they both hold in their hearts for one another. Not even an alligator....Well, okay, they'll beat the alligator's ass so they can back to their love. Y'all get what I mean. The love seems unbreakable.

What if you heard the Lord say, "Simon, Simon! (Place your first name there) Behold, Satan desired to have you, that he may sift you as wheat. But I prayed for you, Simon (put your name there) that your faith may not fail. And when you have turned back, strengthen your brothers."

"Simon, Simon, Satan has asked to sift each of you like wheat. But I have prayed for you, Simon, that your faith will not fail. And when you have turned back, strengthen your brothers." Luke 23:21

Imagine if you heard that before entering into a committed relationship, one that leads to marriage. What would be your response? Worship is one response; proceeding further with caution to intimately discuss with the Lord God is another. Inquire if this is going to be a wheat-sifting relationship.

WHEAT/GRAIN AND CHAFF MEANING:

- To sift as wheat means to separate the grain from the chaff. Sifting wheat from chaff reveals weaknesses.
- To examine all the parts of something closely in order to find something or separate what is useful from what is not.
- In the Bible, when Jesus spoke of sifting, He referred to a

violent action to separate the grain from the stalk and chaff. Using threshing machines like in today's wheat fields tearing the wheat apart, separating the valuable portion from the worthless portion.

In this violent process of sifting in the threshing machines, imagine yourself being sifted to remove all your worthiness and value, leaving you with nothing but worthless portions.

It's not a pretty picture. Being sifted in a relationship by a toxic partner is the same as the wheat. In the latter part of the scripture, Jesus says, but I pray your faith fails you not.

Have you been led to move forward and did not because they purchased flowers and promised never to hit or cheat on you again? Maybe they made new declarations or spoke sweet nothings in your ear? Were you thinking sound, or was it the voice of low self-esteem talking?

What about yourself that made you feel you should stay in a toxic relationship? Do you need to change you, change the way you think?

What you allow in your ear gate to saturate your thoughts and heart will dominate. Don't get me wrong, as women, we desire a man's physical touch (like holding hands or a hug) but emotional clarity causes you to think differently beyond your emotions.

So you stayed, and your faith failed you; I'm not minimizing the decision to stay or leave a toxic relationship. However, faith pleases God; without faith, it's impossible to please Him. Many people have made life decisions based on a one-night stand, adulterous affair, infidelity, and the like. Low self-esteem is a vice that convinces a person to misalign their emotions.

Do you know that God wants you to be happy in healthy relationships? So why not lean into His love, joy, and kindness instead of your own understanding?

LOW SELF-ESTEEM MEANING:

- *Ingrained* negative beliefs a person has about themselves. Stressful life events like toxic relationships can also cause low self-esteem.

- Low self-esteem causes a person to draw back and retreat to a lower version of themselves. Minimizing the sift of worthlessness from a toxic partner.

- Low self-esteem increases health problems like depression, social phobia, substance abuse, or eating disorders.

- Low self-esteem is a silent whisperer in the ears of many, convincing them to remain in a chapter that reinforces negativity.

There is no good fruit production in a manipulative relationship. We are aware that God can do anything; nothing is impossible for Him. Remember the Israelites and Pharaoh? God used Moses to request that Pharaoh let His people go. Even though Moses knew the Biblical truth, Pharaoh did not.

However, God led the Israelites to the Jordan River, where Moses used his rod, which was made from an almond branch. Moses placed his rod toward the water, and God's hands divided and held the water, allowing the Israelites to escape on dry land. Once they crossed the Red Sea, God released the water, and Pharaoh and his army were no more. He dealt treacherously with the Israelites' enemies.

When God tells you to move forward, low self-esteem and the familiar voices of others take a back seat to His directional move for you. It's faith that pushes you to move forward and listen to the instructions from God, the Father, God the Son, and God the Holy Spirit.

The Greek meaning for self-esteem is a deep, profound respect and love for self. It also means:

- Holding yourself in high regard.
- Thinking you are incapable and very critical of themselves.
- To treasure self; do you treasure toxicity above your worth?
- High estimation or value, great regard, favorable opinion.

"To esteem" means sometimes "to think or "reckon" in other connections; it means to regard as honorable or "valuable". When you flee an unproductive and unhealthy chapter, certain weights fall off as described in chapter 3.

"Those who have reverence for the Lord will learn from Him the path they should follow." Psalms 25:12

THINGS TO PONDER

- Think about your strengths and activate movement with it.
- Refrain from beating yourself up. Beating yourself up is wasted energy. Self-hate and being critical of oneself does not go after your weaknesses and pulls on your strength.
- Do things you enjoy!

"The name of the LORD is a fortified tower; the righteous run to it and are safe." Proverbs 18:10

Small Project

Place the following on sticky notes and stick it where you often frequent; Your residence, workplace, vehicle, etc.

I am _____ (you fill in the blank). For example, "I am helpful" or "I am a good leader."

That's wassup! You get the picture; take it from there. Repeat these phrases out loud to reinforce positivity for yourself. This will help rid you of the negative words your spouse, fiancée, and others has sifted you to believe about yourself.

"Beloved, I pray that you may prosper in all things and be in health, just as your soul prospers." 3 John 1:2

Life Through The Lasagna Perspective Lens:

Add to your life, make it **BIGGER**.

The chapter you're fleeing or have fled from has the residue of past attacks that initiate fear, discouragement, bitterness, resentment, and unforgiveness into your soul and spirit.

Your new chapter awaits with fresh aroma and perspective from the Holy Spirit—new direction, sound, friends, and happiness. Beware: Your old chapter cheater will try to slither his way into your new beginning. SILENCE IT IMMEDIATELY! Change all your social media platform statuses and block them if necessary. Refuse to entertain or be entertained by the cheater and other narcissistic men who may come intentionally your way.

Sometimes, you don't need a timer to know your lasagna is ready, as the sauces, melted cheese, and ingredients perfume the kitchen. Discernment is similar to that. So, discern at a greater height in your new chapter.

Decide where you're happy!

~Sam The Lasagna Lady

Chapter Seven

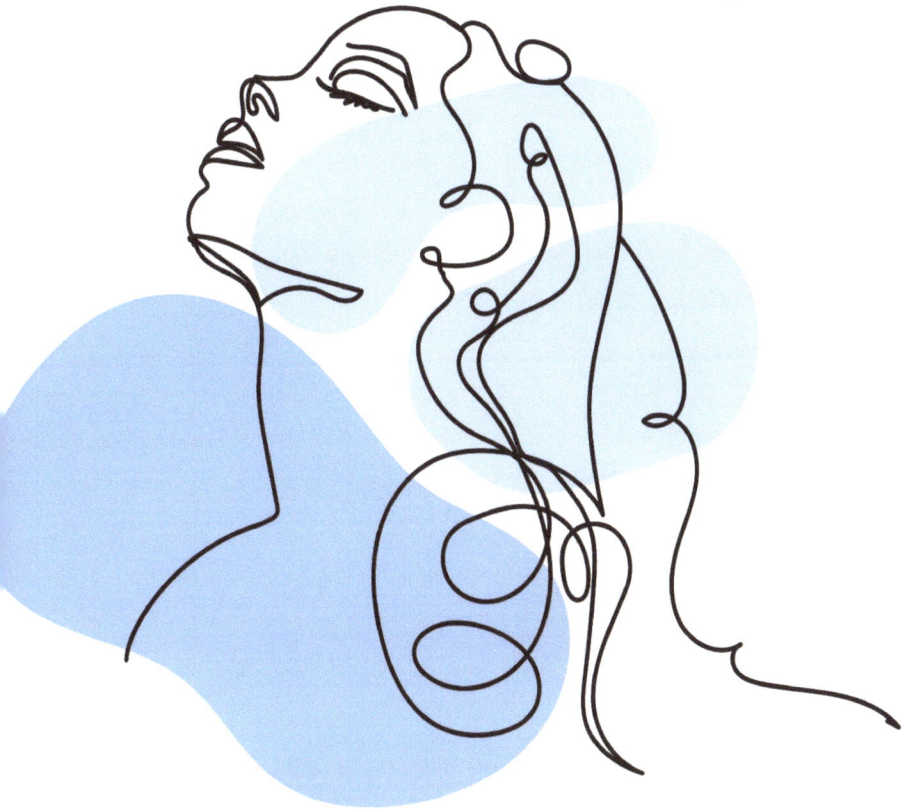

Your Happiness Matters

*Happiness is not a trendy season,
it's a life long promise!"*

*"Step, dance, and jam
in your new Stilettoes!"*

"He who heeds the word wisely will find good, and whoever trusts in the LORD, happy is he." Proverbs 16:20

You may have heard the words bliss, contentment, delight, enjoyment, peace of mind, satisfaction, good cheer, and hopefulness before.

Until this very moment, happiness seemed distant by routine bondage of a toxic relationship(s). Although you have the inner joy broadcasting resilience beyond your situation, happiness is the outer expression.

As I journeyed through being cheated on repeatedly, I wondered if there's one man out there for me that doesn't attribute his greatest asset as a cheater. Is there one who knows how to cover his wife without arrogant control, one who is not phony (masking narcissism), and all that's connected to it? Is there one that simply understands a woman's worth and plays no games with women? ONE!!!

Then I realized that full happiness begins with me. If you are not happy with yourself, change! No one else will be happy with you if you are unhappy with yourself, specifically the man you're with, although he's the cause.

As your situations or trauma drained your memory of happiness accepting a cheater seems normal; Well, everyone's cheating so I guess I'm good, I mean, at LEAST he comes home and takes care of the bills, etc. Not the AT LEAST girl; free yourself from AT LEAST. Cheaters are naturally disrespectful. Maybe not in front of others, but rather behind closed doors, something you are all too familiar with. Your happiness matters without being disrespected by a cheating mf'er.

You were not always living a united front pretending to be happy when you were not. We've all been there, so you are not alone, girl. Put on your mature girl and forgive him, the women or men he cheated with; forgive the relatives in the family that knew and were laughing at you behind your back, yes, even them. Forgive aborted dreams and dream with God for you. He's got big dreams, and He loves you to dream with Him. Lean into God dreaming for you.

Your happiness is linked to this forgiveness. Forgive yourself, have a 10-minute cry, and move forward. Purchase several journals that speak to you and write in them every day, if you can. If you don't know where to start, begin with gratitude.

Write down what you're grateful for and how you feel. Talk about your favorite color and why. Jot down what success means to you. Those are a few ideas of many to begin your journal entries.

If you are an avid journal writer, advance to turning that journal into a book or memoir. Take your writing to another dynamic. Allow God to speak to you on what that means for you. Happiness comes in many forms, but first, start by being happy with yourself.

"Trust in the Lord with all your heart and lean not onto your own understanding. In all your ways submit to Him, and he will make your paths straight." Proverbs 3:5-6

Trust is directional. You can choose to trust yourself, your cheating spouse, or the Lord. Happiness has notes of trust in it and can be defined as such:

- Happiness differs across cultures, and it is an overall appreciation of one's life as a whole.
- Self-acceptance: What you like and dislike. Being fully aware of your strengths and weaknesses. Focusing too much on

your weaknesses does not build your strengths.

- Personal Growth: Finding out you married a cheater can be a blessing. Now, you can move forward if you decide to. The fact that you know this is that you have outgrown his ass, and there is no need to waste any time with him; discover and improve yourself, and keep your focus close to God. Discover adventures, skills, observations, and new encounters, and welcome God-ordained friendships.

There's much to discover about the powerful new you. Your happiness matters and is truly a blessing from God. So, welcome it! Begin your day by speaking to it. Talk to God about your day; He delights to hear from you. Tell Him about your pain, fears, joys, and whatever your heart desires to talk about. He is a great listener.

As you journal your happiness, be brave enough to let go of people who do you no good and welcome those that are genuinely for you. Being wiser is a form of happiness.

You now know the difference between short-term relationships and relationships that are a lifetime; being surrounded by people that "got cho back" is awesome!

Your cheater is a naysayer. You know what this looks like, so stay away from those who speak negatively of you.

Meaningful relationships are important in your season of growth and discovery of the powerful new you. Pursue goals you tucked away years ago and bring them back to life with a new perspective and meaning. Rather, you skip, play double-dutch, run a marathon, write a book(s), travel the world, feed the homeless, paint, or listen to a new genre of music. Do what makes you happy; the happiest, your new you bring. As I write this chapter, I'm listening to the following song: *Martin Ikin & Sammy Porter – Back To Funk (blanc)*. That's one song that makes me happy!!!!!!

THINGS TO PONDER

- Do what makes you happy!
- Rescue you from betrayal and pursue God. Find out your purpose and lean heavily into it.
- Laugh often!!! Laugh often again!!!
- Eat a balanced meal and nestle it with proper sleep.
- Maintain your budget. Financial Peace University is a good resource as there are many others. I only can share the one I attended twice virtually. The cost is feasible and a good investment into the new powerful you.
- Follow through on your goals, girls, even if it's just getting some pens and notebooks to begin organizing something.
- Love on yourself. Send yourself a gift card or gift each month in the mail to yourself.
- **"The blessing of the LORD makes one rich, And He adds no sorrow with it."** Proverbs 10:22

Life Through The Lasagna Perspective Lens

Bathe in the dish of your dreams. Of course, I'm talking about the things you've always dreamed about from the perspective of the dish of my expertise, Lasagna. Make your dream a reality, then dream again and make that even bigger, taller, and as wide as your dream takes you. Lasagna can be built as wide as your imagination, and as tall as your dreams. After you've dreamed, and dreamed and dreamed, DREAM AGAIN!

**Like Lasagna, your dreams have a way of evolving.
Meaningful Relationships Are Organic.**

~Sam The Lasagna Lady™

Thaank You!

I found healing and inspiration when writing this guide. Telling myself to Get The Hell Up! gave me the bravery needed to flee a toxic relationship. I cried and laughed, then cried some more, then laughed again. I realized that external united fronts are a classic factor in being with a cheater.

After getting the hell up, my first night at the Hotel was unloaded with the weight I carried from his cheating. God removed the weight; I thank Him for giving me the courage to move forward, His amazing love, friendship, and more.

When I arrived at the Hotel, homeless, two friends of mine, Sylvester and Miranda Dean, prayed for me outside the hotel. No one could break the circle of prayer as they locked their hands with mine and prayed. Everything around stood still until Sylvester finished praying. I embraced them both and thanked them for taking time out to pray for me. Thank you both for being the married couple you are and for your friendship. Your words of empowerment are cherished.

Living at the hotel for over one month, I got to know a new family of friends. They know I had to have my late-night Frito's (Lol). With tears of joy, thank you, Hilton Hotel staff, for your hospitality, love, and spirit of excellence. Thanks, Matt, for tips on the game we love. Not to mention Saltine's dishes. One week, I had the same meal at least 3 or 4 times; somebody stopped me! It was delicious. Thanks, Saltine, for your professionalism and that yummy catch of the day. Which brings me to Varia, damn it, Chef Aaron, that Chicken Parmesan is off the chart. I enjoyed that dish so many times that I stopped counting during my stay. Chef, we still need to swap recipes...Lol. And the late-night meals at the Grain after long days, thank you, Chassity and others on the team. Coupled with the warmth of the front desk ambassadors, Rebecca in housekeeping made my stay there beyond exceptional. Before I knew who she was, Rebecca would place my personal blanket a certain way, which I loved. Each time I entered my room, I knew it was that lady. That lady is what I called her before knowing her name. She even made a swan with a bath towel without knowing what brought me to the hotel. It just added a certain ambiance to the Hotel brand.

Thanks, Rebecca, for that; it really helped me on the days I needed a friend. Many thanks to Nikki and Cynthia, to name a few, for your hospitality. Sabre, Rebecca, Maya, Chenna, Michael, Ron (thanks for the Fritos), Marketa, Leslie, Cody, Michael, Sakita, Julius, LaCretia, Rosemary, Eddie, and Marquis, ya'll ROCK! If I had to name ya'll as a rap group, you'd be like A Tribe Called Quest, Pete Rock and CL Smooth. Ya'll get the picture. Thanks for all the conversations; I'm grateful for that. And Marquis, save me some Fritos, Lol.

To my new additonal fam! Carson, Lindsey, Gabriel, thank you for being there for me. Eric, Dereck, and Marie, thank you for every thing you do.

To Renee and Lee, all I can say is thank you. You both give me hope for a healthy marriage and the man God has for me.

And to Sheila, Paige, Polly, Suzzane (Sulka), Bainy Cyrus author of Tea & Toil, At The Woman's Club; Beverly, Monica and the WCN family, I thought about you reached out to me when I walked away from a toxic marriage; the value of your words and love and how y'all showed up, God showed out! Words cannot express the beauty you GALS bring to other women, especially the heart felt love I receive from you.

M, M's; You know who you are. Thanks for encouringing me and being as fruitful as you are.

I have layers of thanks to my publisher, Felicia Benton, for taking those early morning calls before you had your coffee, for your friendship, and for your ability to extract the good from your authors and publish uniquely. Momma, Momma, Bahama, Momma, your mom for always telling us the truth about men who don't know how to treat a good thing, their wife. **Ladies, let music play in your heart again; it'll be worth the wait!**

It's unnatural to remain in an environment accepting the the manipulation of a cheater. You know he's cheating, whether married or not. Your worth is being tested, and your cheater is fully aware. He knows that you'd rather devalue yourself as a woman instead of stepping out on faith beyond his cheating ass and being the big badass woman that he's afraid of. You've carried the weight of his women while you waited in hope for change. Still, you are weighed down with promises and the heaviness of infidelity. Girl, this is your Get the Hell Up guide!

A man knows he can play several women simultaneously because some ladies don't ask questions. They assume because he asks how you slept the night before, the how r u? text messages, or no texts at all for days or weeks, then you got the nerve to respond to his insecure ass as though he is worthy of your attention. Wrong, he is not! Your value is far greater; to hell with his cheating, insecure, don't know how to be a man or treat a woman ass.

You can shut it down by not entertaining a man who plays games with women. But be careful, they are master manipulators, so they know how to get in a woman's head.

I don't know about your relationship with God. However, lean into His love and allow Him to lead, guide, and reveal your purpose.

Girl, this is your guide to Get The Hell Up!

From the humble pasta noodle to the grandeur of baked lasagna, Chef Samantha Peavy, known as Sam The Lasagna Lady, has left an indelible mark. Her unique perspective, which she calls the "Life throug lasagna lens," has not only influenced and inspired but also transformed numerous businesses and thousands of lives. Her prophetic strategy, mentoring, media appearances, and books are all testament to her innovative approach.

As a prophetic thought strategist, she spent over 27 years as a lasagna expert. Samantha has a superior ability to lean into what she calls the lasagna lens, solve problems, and help businesses and others. She helps individuals, entrepreneurs, and business leaders move beyond their reach to build a new dynamic from the inside out by applying her unique strategy layering techniques.

Through her techniques, Sam's creativity, and innovative solutions to living past an individual's why. Samantha's process rediscovers imagination in repurposing the pasta noodle to life application. Guided by her passion for lasagna, Sam has developed many recipes for the entrée, which grew from three iterations in her grassroots beginnings as owner of Sam's Gourmet Lasagna. With countless hours of volunteering with Ronald McDonald's House in Hyde Park, Chicago, going under bridges at night, and giving away lasagna to homeless individuals, she now is a member of the Women's Club of Norfolk, where they honor local municipal and the entire community through Love & Lasagna during different seasons.

One of Samantha's quotes is, "When Life Throws You Lemons, Make Lasagna." She authored Life Through Lasagna Eyes: The Recipes for Life & Book Strategy Manual (Layering Book Writing Through Lasagna). Both books display Samantha's personality, talent, and gift for the extraordinary, using her expertise to look through the lens of lasagna. Her take on layering lasagna and rediscovering imagination is one of the tools she shares to help individuals grow and strengthen their capacity in the World.

He Cheated: Get The Hell Up guide, Samantha shares unique perspectives at the end of each chapter.

"Lasagna has a way of bouncing back."
"Ever had this dish on the second day, and it tasted better than the first? This book is your bounce-back day. Elevate your purpose; smile inside; that's your strength".
~Sam The Lasagna Lady

www.ingramcontent.com/pod-product-compliance
Lightning Source LLC
Chambersburg PA
CBHW041218270326
41931CB00001B/24